Sensual, tender, widened, messy, you.

By Dom Demming

I dedicate this book to our

humanity and the fuckery in us all.

I hope you make all the messes and live

to tell about it.

P.S.. I dare you to rip out any of these pages that speak to you

and make art with it by hanging it up in a weird frame

you found at goodwill or put it in a collage.

let it live beyond the page

Discomfort in velvet

If you avoid discomfort,

you miss the possibility to get to know the

you that is discomfort dressed in velvet like skin.

Goggly Moogly eyes

Let your feet be your unidentified witness,

Let nature be your unidentified witness,

let the air be your unidentified witness,

Let the sensation that formulates into goosebumps allowing

you this resonance to how your body commands to speak be

your unidentified witness,

let the melody of your music playlists be your unidentified

witness,

let your pen that is gripped tightly in the palm of your hand

with your fingers reaving up like a loud engine be your

unidentified witness,

Let your ears hear the conversations your desert of a mouth is

desperately trying to get out be an unidentified witness,

Let your nose scope out the smells of your own bullshit and

be a unidentified witness.

The Puritan pipe dream

There is such a vice to being clean, pure, fresh.

Holy, all of the time.

You can't force yourself out of the sticky or stringy

even if you light sage or stick a crystal up your ass,

Believe me, I have tried...does a crystal

glass wand count as sticking something

somewhere?

I have tried to rid myself clean and there the

aromatic tangy smell still orbiting around me.

Sometimes the actual requirement is staying in the dirt,

 sleeping with grief as a mistress,

romancing the dark, murky stench of a shadow,

howling like the ravenous wolf you are and punching the nearest pillow,

asking annoying why's like a curious child,

crying like an inconsolable faucet, stepping in muddy

 puddles and deciding to spatter it around

and licking pleasure like a spatula with homemade batter.

Until another cycle of you is summoned into another go round.

I was called a pessimist once

" you are such a realist" she said

and because when you linger with watching depressing shit

have jalapeño hot Cheeto dust stained fingers and when you play the sad,

acoustic, low-fi songs over and over again

you are doomed to being beige and boring

when playing the sad songs over and over again--open my chest and consume

the tar like goo around my heart that demands to be sewn all the way up like my

grandmother's sweater.

its uncomfortable to admit that those songs make me hold myself in tension or

the real soaked truth that I an so painfully alive in every moment I feel emotion.

Sometimes I hate it.

I like to listen to music like that over and over--it's ritualistic.

To keep playing on repeat until I can listen without feeling a thing.

It's my form of therapy when I don't want anyone to witness me--myself included.

watching depressing shows or a sad movie that slowly turns me on like a knob

on a slurpy machine from a generic gas station: circulating through to drop down the delicious,

soft, fluffy, frozen drink just as my tears drip out of my eyes, ..I can't hide.

Those types of movies and shows give me a home to allow all

of humanness to actually roam even if some parts of me choose to close the door.

Maybe I am a realist... I don't know.

I refuse to just believe in the happy, holy, gunk.

I want to color in the lines of the opposite funk, that I hear pairs well

with a tall glass of fuck and a you and to anyone else who has an opinion of you.

When they can take a number with the rest of the round table that lives inside our heads.

Creativity IS intimacy

into--me--see

It makes sense as to why

you may want to abandon it,

 avoid it, question it,

suffocate & cling to it or try to eagerly control it.

It's so tender, small and wide.

its exposing & shame at any time

can ram it's big head right into it.

I hope you have the big kahunas to choose the terrifying

longevity --to practice forming a love affair

with your own creativity.

Don't get so clouded by the bulging neon light sign

 coming out of your head

that you see every time you are in a

mirror or a new wrinkle appears

or when taking a photo saying, "holy fuck, you are old

when approaching the

avalanche of becoming 30, 40, 50, 70 years old"

I know, it's there but don't

 forget about 28, 45, 52 or 69.

They deserve your living too.

I can't fathom to count how many times I have heard,

" don't cry"

as if I would somehow combust into a pea mush

of nothings or

have a parking spot reserved

that reads, "she is disappointingly weak"

Tears are compost

and when did weak need to be met with the categorical

 label of bad or less than?

weak is as mysterious as a dark cave and

 vast as an ocean.

Your form is a glass vase in a human ,

fragile but not decayed,

Your sustenance belongs to rest, living out emerged

questions and allowing the silhouette of silence

to catch your gaze.

your skin and strained body becomes the

soil that extracts

Weak one or weak one in their moments,

they didn't dare tell you that this is where your

 own efficiency of the self emerges.

Curiosity will lead you

call upon it but don't chokehold it--it is not a destination.

Sometimes it feels as if I am an overcast.

I want to disappear, maybe live out the fantasy of

being a hag in the woods.

I want to disappear, more often lately.

I'm questioning everything,

Who I am

why I want to continue on here.

I still have yet to find the particular answer.

Can I be okay without an actual formulated answer?

Can I be not okay without an actual formulated answer?

Why do I choose to asphyxiate my dangling in the air

 existence for an answer?

When I know my stubborn self will challenge that too.

What if I'm just looking for myself or more so

the fragmented parts of what

makes up me in a heaping pile of cultured "supposed to be's"

I took my shoes off as I walked into

the field area that's next to the parking lot.,

clouds were loud and in between my toes. the grass brushed.

I laughed.

i'm ticklish and my hips started to sway,

my arms, my chest all mimicking my hips in

movement. The wind-my dance partner.

All I could think about was how when I move, open my mouth

as if it could spread just like a bird with its wings--

you give earth right back to herself

when you allow yourself to just exist.

Have you tried recycling yourself yet?

Touch grass, feel the dirt between your

fingers to emerge

out the

hollowness

of the dark forrest that

masks itself as your mind

-- go recycle yourself and come back.

IDENTITIES

My mother has been going through BII (breast implant illness)

with her health for over a year.

I want to take a machete and cut off the parts of me

 that are worried, angry at the beauty tornado that

rips out natural foundations --

whole and replaces it with artificial injections and

sculpted looks--

I don't know if it was the snickering of

 unknown death that blasted my ears or

 maybe the truth-- I don't know my

mother beyond that identity.

My mother had explant surgery --

 releasing silicone toxins off of her chest.

she took my hand and led me into her heart.

I met Claudia

I spent 4 hours on phone calls hearing her valid ,

anxiety filled stories, her guilt about men,

her vapid shame-- I saw mirrors of my own self in her.

I occupied the last stall in many bathrooms with her

 during nighs' out: holding the terrifying realizations of

 her taking layer by

layer of hardened skin that she proclaimed as her--

 to carving a space that

submerges her into who she gets to be now

holding her in imploding grief of what she

made the implants mean about being a woman.

Parallels that formed a bridge of complex

understanding why the doorway into my

 childhood was neurotic and painful--

she was a child raising one too.

I don't like admitting how alike we actually are--is it weird

to say that feels too intimate?

Before I existed, she did.

As her own person

I was there during the beginning of her womanhood.

As I grew, she did too.

I'm scared to be this close to her.

the day before her surgery, I told her how brazen she is.

I didn't tell her I imagined her in this wide, completely open field,

frockling and spinning with this big cheesy grin, arms flowing

with the light wind, while the long rusty daggers of ageism,

self misogyny

and the epitome of our culture for women were trying to

 deeply penetrate into the

wounds that were never hers to carry alone.

she created this force field of ferocity and I know every single

ancestor was back to back with her in awe of what she did

 for her own self.

She makes me want to be more brave

in my own autotomy.

I am still processing and walking with the child and teenager
inside; home to adult me

this connection is what I longed for and want to fervently push out

I asked all kinds of questions; " how did you and dad meet?"

" did you think you weren't worthy of the love that is kind--is that

what made you run from it?"

" did you ever regret me since you had me at 19? "

" where did you go when you snuck out of grammy's house?"

my heart stretched and I cannot help it but savor this all up like its

the last part of sucking an after dinner mint before it becomes

nothing on your tongue

Life gets busy

& sometimes it demands all of your attention

take space to ask those questions beyond just the identities you

know that person you are thinking about right now as.

don't let them live in the void

what's their name?

<u>Start there.</u>

What if you allowed yourself to be so full on yourself?

Full of your own breath,

full of your movement,

full of your heart,

full of your ever contradicting

truth in moments you occupy,

full of belief or the delusion of it,

full of your own nourishment-- food or your own hands,

full on grace for your own humanity,

full on the murkiness

that makes up the outline of your shadow,

full on being frisky for the mystery,

so so so full that opinions can't starve you of yourself.

It takes permission

permission is the jolting tingle

that lingers up into your back when the palm of

your own hand snacks your own ass.

permission stings.

permission asks you to play in the translucent

faith and give yourself like an offering to courage.

permission is a slow, elongated breathe.

Permission releases and it also takes.

Permission is a canal; giving you more

seeds that move within you like a vertebrate.

Allow permission to lure you in.

Allow it to anoint you to yourself again and again.

Grief sometimes will feel like a callus.

A hardened layer of skin that formed out of

protection due to the friction you endured.

What if you allowed grief to have its way with you?

Allowing it to be exposed, tenderizing it and softening it

until it alchemizes itself into a teacher.

SELFIE

" I don't remember the last time I--shush" I said to myself
as my left hand laid gently on my top lip,
grabbing my phone with the other & decided.
Today, that's the day I adore & feast my eyes back on me."

The art of changing

The human skin replenishes itself once a month, underneath

your visible vessel,

every other layer of you takes two weeks

It makes sense to change

your body continually does that

unapologetically and lives.

It's okay to change your mind.

I don't want to strive and chase only happiness

Happiness to me, is this fleeting experience.

I want to be alive.

My heart completely engorged and stretched like taffy

from how uncomfortably open I am,

I want to be so alive in joy that I am scared to close my eyes

that I might miss it entirely.

I want to feel my sadness filling my chest like a sunken ship.

I want to simintaously feel the pain that dissects my brain

and feel grace as a balm soothing my insides.

I want to be alive.

I want to feel so terrifyingly intimate with my sex,

be consumed by the gnawing Oxytocin in my cells

 that travel

the map of my body and pussy--leaving me

 empty and weeping

in both our presence for the art of connection.

I want to be alive.

I want to cry unbashfully. I want to be

exposed and cradled in my lover's arms

and feel these little ghostly arms of my

 inner child join in the embrace--it

becomes alchemical and creates honey

into my whole body and watch it

drip out to feed the stinging of bees that

occupy my mouth and nervous system.

I want to be so alive.

I want to be so fucking alive.

That is something to solemnly live for.

**Being
alive
IS
the
occasion**

4am and I couldn't sleep

anxiety stirring in my chest

I sat up and placed my lavender body pillow

behind me and leaned my back and shoulders into it

Closing my eyes tightly,

as tears are trying to gouge out

making a trail down my left cheek

I think this is called relief

Belly

Sucking it in.

passing mirrors, windows of parked cars, when I go into a

restaurant, when I get up to push a chair in for precaution anyone

seeing me from a side angle, when I lay completely naked from

being fucked, sitting, standing, when I laugh, when I am on top,

when I am looking at other women's bodies--

why am I so turned off by my fullness anyway?

I wish one of the things I did more-explode

in abraded emotion

in no's

in uncontrollable laughter.. body jolting backward

while my head yanks back without covering my

gap in my tooth or playing it "cool" to appear more collected.

I want more expression on my face when things taste gross or sour or sweet

and not care about how they make wrinkles

licking my fingers from cool ranch Doritos

I don't want to Tighten my reactions

I'm going to explode

like lava chocolate cake--

a slow burn

taking over

to remind me I am free here

to implode.

I still push and push

to prove to myself that eventually you'll leave too...

somehow thinking that will dress me up in ease..

isn't that me--showing my own self to abandon any

ounce of love that wants to turn itself into a lodge

 to be called home?

And when you think of your hands,

may you remember you are a lover of

you, too.

I once told my brother
"slow it down.. take your time... whatever the word or sound it is...
is what it is... I trust your pain and I trust what you are saying"
and I thought to myself,
when was the last time I told my
own itchy body and bratty brain that
when it's screaming to be heard?

You

make

complexity

look

hot

Give me patience

when I want to metamorphose into

boxing gloves and you have hands

made of soft, fresh flowers

and a molasses mouth.

I'm not used to genuine affection without it

carrying a bouquet of manipulation.

Even if it makes absolutely no sense,

it does eventually

become the sense in the making

**when the culture monster or the 30's haunt or
your mother asks what you are doing
or when you feel this confusion around purpose:**

Your purpose isn't in what you do,

your purpose is in who you are, existing of,

widening, weaving in

 and out of as you get to know

the findings of your own interested

enjoyment, being seduced and dragged

by the mystery that straddles curiosity

you are already your purpose in motion,

moment to moment.

self seeking self

I don't want to love myself

I don't want to love myself, I want to feast and love being myself.

Loving myself ironically had a thread of me sifting through

 my body & my mind to search for all of the scavenger hunt like hurt

or improvement to attend the event of approving loving myself.

when I say, I want to love being myself, I didn't rummage or plead-I

started to understand the intelligence all over me.

I saw more of my quirks,

I asked myself, " what can make today interesting?

What makes me interested to be here?

Where can I enjoy and

 also hold the spot for the objectifying shame

bubble that wants to rubble like my tummy

when I ate something "bad"?

Can I love being who I am in this moment and the next moment...

the moody,

the overstimulated,

the seductive vixen,

the grief struck processor,

dramatic big feeler,

the amnesiac mystical beast,

the one who doesn't even want to leave the damn bed of thornes,

the obnoxious dancer in the kitchen,

the messy creator,

the bratty, tantrum like muse.

all of it.

the humanity part in us all.

is me.

is you.

Can you love being yourself?

Even when the shame comes knocking.

Even when you feel like a microcosm of a human.

In the movies,

when the main character is having their contemplation scene

with the saddest acoustics

They become a stand still in a time lapse

and that's me

I have become sewn in by tears and blood and anger and grief

with the couch, the cold white tiled kitchen floor and laying on

the left side of my bed, looking at the sliding door with the

peeks of sun coming in that sting my skin

as the world continues to blur

Im so mad that it didn't get to know you

Im so mad no one came running through the front door with

pitch forks and fire raging at

the devastation that you didn't get to live.

May I not rot in bitterness too long

May I allow my grief and anger to remind me of how much I

love you and how alive I am for the sake of you.

for you... I'll live.

**–Miscarriages and abortions are
valid of grief and shame and all the other things**

You are early.

You are early.

You are early.

--When you think are too late

I stare and pull my tummy as if its playdo

contorting and squeezing

Trying to somehow mold it into what I think I still need to look like

my belly button

still stays right in the center of me

turning left or right

becoming a half fold of my body

your belly Botton

a birthing scar

I think of it as the actual landmark of you

there is nothing like it

its the only thing that is the absolute proof you exist

outside of a womb

your first breathe. comes close to second

if its there. and its the remebernace of us

that means you cannot be erased

or eroded from your own

epicenter

you are the core

the atom

the cosmic beam

always close

and there

place your palms and fingers on it

and remember

take a breath

and start right here

at the center of you

again.

I knew I loved you when we were teens, you searched your truck for quarters for the nearest dollar menu to makeshift it into a car date. I knew I loved you when I puked outside of your car window and I was crying feeling the embarrassment warming my cheeks and you told me, " baby, its fine, I'm glad you did it outside." I knew I loved you when I hung up the phone in disbelief from the first time you told me you loved me and you waited patiently as you gave me space to process--you were the first person that has ever said it and meant it. I knew I loved you when you saw me cry even with every thrust of my hands for not accepting your embracing arms, you gently pulled me into your chest to know I was held. I knew I loved you when we had the windows down on a hot Arizona summer night, hearing the cicadas while blasting a song as the heat whipped our faces--you found a song that reminded you of us. I knew I loved you when I got my tampon stuck and you willingly pulled it out of me and we deep belied laughed on my bedroom floor. I knew I loved you when you stayed when I mistook discomfort as a chance to channel Forrest Gump and run because I was taught that when that happens, its ending and I thought I wasn't enough for your big squishy love when it was another layer of intimacy beggining between us. You still stayed. I knew you loved me when you looked into my eyes on our first morning together from moving in and crying the night before because we are big adults now on our own--rolling over, you looked deep into my eyes and put your nose against mine and told me how beautiful I am with the little light spots coming in from the curtain. I knew I loved you when you told me my words matter and the way I live deserves to be told. I knew I loved you when I'm writing this and its 2am, your playlist of jazz music is on and you made us grilled cheeses and cut mine into a triangle because I feel so weird if It isn't that... I knew I loved you... and I still do.

I keep reading " your body is art" and I do believe that

I needed to show myself I am.

I bought a white poster board and painted it black

I got into my thong and gently taking a wide paintbrush

dipped it in hot pink paint all over my ass

as it graced it, I couldn't help but laugh at the coldness

from the stroke of the brush.

Covering my whole back side and upper thigh

I slowly squatted down onto the posterboard

sandwiched together, the poster board and I

moving my lower half

in small circles to make sure the paint got my imprint

Gripping the sides of the couch next to me

to help pull me up

I ran quickly to the shower to wash off

not knowing if I got it or not

wrapping myself in a yellow towel

I leaned over my art of myself

and I was in awe.

voluptuous.

how bright the paint glowed over my curves

I had to put on my ruby red lipstick and kiss

the top left corner and sign it

yes, my body is art

and this art is making an

artifact out of me.

every picture or painting or video or pose you do

becomes your electric retelling of witnessing yourself

blooming the observer of the messy and brilliant

and embarrassing landscape you navigated on.

I put the painting above my TV in my bedroom

When I lay on my bed, I look directly at it.

I'm worthy of being on my own display

and you are worthy of capturing

the museum of you..

your body is the met gala of art

The most erotic thing you can do is....

love your

ACHY, CONFUSING, MESSY, HUMANNESS.

when I write,
" I don't know what I want to say"
" I definitely don't feel like writing"
is the thing you can start with,
and when I get
stuck or I critique what I wrote
and makes my pen now flaccid
I start from that line,
" I don't know what to say"
What if the pages, the computer
screen, your blue blockers,
your notepad in your phone
get to hold you as you are?
write right there.

The death of us

I lingered my finger over our last text thread, this inner twisting in my stomach as if it was a wet towel needing to be squeezed out- wanting to say something but back spacing any word that formulated out. Sometimes the thing you need to do for yourself no matter how aligned or good or thoroughly thought out of a decision it is: it can still smell like shame.

It doesn't mean it's necessarily wrong ti may be the uncomfortability of wearing your own autonomy around your neck and allowing yourself off of a hook where you can no longer reel in and: try to throw yourself deeply into the murky water of someone else's ocean to try to make them understand.

I have had a continuous and very turbulent relationship with my mother in law.

I fantasized a lot of it. Parts of me wanted to be loved by another potential mother figure. Any silvers that felt like my mom didn't give me, I unknowingly placed upon her like an invisible crown. I wanted to belong to be able to bond with another mother who can accept me. When I would watch movies, I was so enamored on the whole mother and daughter in law relationship that further kept that fantasy alive within me.

I do believe that's why I excused a lot of her harmful behavior, holding onto any grace that maybe she could change. I denied who she kept showing me was because in the back of my heart, I felt empathy for the trauma she endured in her life. We can't excuse someone else's trauma and allow it to be a hall pass when they are leaking their pain all on us to project and point fingers of blame. It becomes a form of self harm when we abandon our own pain from bypassing another.

I don't know if it's because I'm almost 30 or I allowed myself to suddenly rub my eyes to clear the blurry-ness or have acknowledged my own accountability over the years but I finally see her for who she is. And I know that I couldn't continue on in fetishizing an illusion connection that never existed at all. I had to and still in moments: grieve her.

grieve the fantasy

grieve the invisible bond.

grieve the " siting on the couch and talking about our lives, getting to her own stories" or being able to invite her into big moments in my personal life or moments in her son and I's lives.

You can't save people, no matter how much love, space, care, resources or trying to understand their own humanity you give them. Especially when they devalue your own humanity and lack empathy and don't partake in their own accountability. Over the years, I have heard, " its your future mother in law, give her grace" no, its not on you nor I to keep constantly extending ourselves to anyone who doesn't at least want to communicate and somatically relate to what we are bringing to them about what has hurt us.

Sometimes the most loving and accepting thing is letting go and grieving a person who still is living.

Sometimes the most loving and accepting thing is allowing yourself to uphold your boundaries because boundaries are yours to hone and meet outward even if it means embodying Edward scissorhands to cut the thread between. As I back space one more time, I took a deep breath, I decided that I didn't have anything else to say. I have said enough to where my mouth felt like a desert.

I clicked her name in my phone,

scrolled down and officially hit the block button.

I deleted the thread and I let out a big sigh.

My chest slowly went down and I cried.

I knew this was the death of us.

the more I realize our bodies are nature--

if you think about your veins

they resemble roots of the strongest trees

I feel weird during environmental springs

I feel more internally like winter

be your season

that transition to one season to a

nother takes adjustment

and I have plenty attempts of trying to

unroll myself like a fruit roll up

of shame thinking why can't I embrace what

the outside is feeling and I feel indifferent.

be your season

anoint yourself with sap like its grace

you forgetful and capable forrest of a human.

stay unapologetically Tender

stay unapologetically Tender

stay unapologetically Tender

I have this theory when you realize you have gained weight

the immediate reaction is Fuck.. and followed with

" how in the fuck..."

and you automatically think it correlates to

bad and need to get rid of

the theory is

what if the weight you gain

was comfort?

from the loved one you shockingly lost

or you letting yourself not make your body

the calculator of food

and enjoyed yourself to where your body is showing you

how nourished it is?

What If its joy?

what if its acceptance that your body let go of something

and every cell celebrated you for that space you now get to widen?

weight gain isn't all the influencers and the trendy

 diet fad makes it out to be

during times of any uncertainty or genuine enjoyment--

it holds you.

Can you stop acting as if practicing, experimenting, moving,
failing, tenderizing is this small mediocre thing you do
when it's a big and small and courageous
paradoxical thing you do?
you are a big, alive and decadent human s
ubstance that lives to tell about it.

Dance it through

fuck it through

feel it through

grieve it through

write it through

scream it through

sing it through

rage it through

believe it through

trust it through

celebrate it through

I was out having a night drive at 1 am, barely anyone

on the highway and at the end of my playlist on Spotify

it brought in suggestions

and the song, next to me by Rufus Du Sol came on

 and reminded me of how I dedicated it

to you.

I let out a grunt and rolled my eyes trying to

quickly turn the song to something else

why does that have to be yours too?

you already got my kindness,, my painting and

my favorite top

it doesn't resemble you

Why do I dedicate these songs I love to people

who don't love me when I need them?

maybe that is a therapy question

I parked in my parking spot, the engine still going

and I decided no

all these songs that once was the melody I heard you in

I'm taking them back

for me

I'm going to put the hottest photo as the cover

 of this new playlist

dedicating them all to me

getting drunk on the love

that you never had the fucking guts to give to me

It's a privilege to be loved by you.

its a privilege to bare witness to your evolution.

Its a privilege to experience you-- fully, alive and dripping.

you are a privilege not ever a guarantee.

SALIVA

let the taste of me

linger in your mouth,

swish me around,

swirl the drop of me around your nude wide tongue,

swallow me whole,

make us one.

Put more flowers in your

bedroom because it's an altar too.

I yearn to remain in the middle

choosing is my strongest weakness

I don't know if that's still the chronic people pleaser in me

that aggressively smoothers herself like a pillow

in the possibility of disappointing people that I give no

recollection to the person who gets the most

disappointment--me

If I choose, I have to own it,

rough edges

mistakes that can be disguised as kerosene

making me want to

turn my body into a U-turn to withstand the subtle heat.

I can choose again and again and again.

That's the ironic synergy of choices.

they go on-- fucking it up or not.

you still chose something

instead of dangling. in dust

like an unused ceiling fan.

make a choice and then choose again.

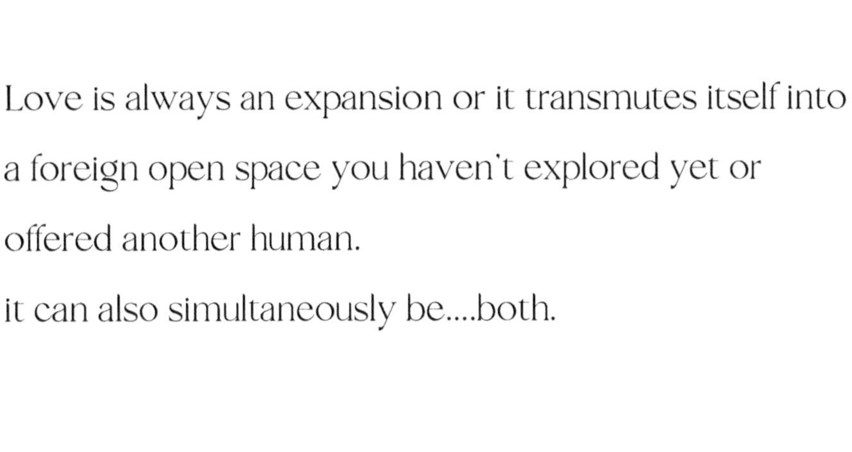

Love is always an expansion or it transmutes itself into

a foreign open space you haven't explored yet or

offered another human.

it can also simultaneously be....both.

I traveld up north to the mountains, every tree on the highway

shedding green and birthing out yellowish hues-- I knew fall

was coming.

The air felt lighter, breathable, clean.

It reminded me of your

vanilla and hazelnut

perfume. I went into the downtown area in flagstaff,

the trees half bare.

Next to the city's used bookstore, there was a

 mural of a woman with

auburn hair, almond shaped green eyes and cool tone skin--

you haunt

in the most random places huh? I remember how we talked

about that being

your next color you do. Consumed by the thought of you,

a burst of wind

billowed around me, my hair blowing up in my face--

that's just like you.

closing my eyes to have your face play like a projection

I wanted to reach my right index finger out to

retrace over your plump, beige lips

again but there was nothing--exactly how you left me in 2019.

with nothing.

I crave a warmth so deep and vigorous--

I haven't felt that since I was

surrounded by amniotic fluid in the womb

The biggest scam the world ever told you

was you needed to be completely healed to summon yourself

whole

You are a continued happening

dying

breaking

fucking

breathing

loving

and being

into every morsel that makes up the entirety of you

Allow

my

hips

to tell

you

stories

Sometimes it's poetry.

Sometimes it's dance.

Sometimes it's a warm, soft blanket.

Sometimes it's re-watching a sad

movie to have you burst

 like a gnarly pimple to remember that it's okay to feel again.

Sometimes it't lighting candles as you

warm up dinner in your

microwave.

sometimes it's turning all the lights off and being in complete

silence to hear yourself. Sometimes it's your

own fingertips tip toeing themselves all over

your body to awaken the sleepy

parts of

your sensual tenderness. Sometimes it's

welcoming in the slow down. Whatever it is...

You are the artistry.

The decay that may be here, right now in this cycle--

know its turning itself into compost.

the grittier the process

 the richness in the soil.

It's okay

If you are unlearning apart of yourself that everyone

has seemed to grasp for themselves a while ago.

its still a celebration.

its still a breathe.

its still a movement.

its still a tending to.

You cannot avoid being misunderstood

it's the honorary badge of expression

Whenever the round table in my head tells me I'm behind or don't know what I'm doing I try to remember I have been cooking.

tenderizing. It doesn't necessarily matter how many days, months, years in between the spaces of my art. No one knows your process like you do. How tedious and messy it is--You have been beautifully and terrifyingly cooking.

and it doesn't diminish your capability.

it has, will and continue to be here.

Marination makes food fall off the bone and so juicy that it can't help itself by dripping all over the plate.

When amnesia strikes again-- you have been _cooking_.

You will disappoint people and maybe you'll feel that by the sudden change you make for yourself and I think that is also called grief and maturity. Allow it to have its way with you and pivot anyway.

Let the rough drafts of your life--

be your bones.

"Your body is forgiving" I said to myself

all week as I was fighting a severe infection.

Your body is very forgiving.

in weight. in stimming, in process, in stretch marks,

in forgetting and circling back around to

what you needed to do,

in emotion, in nasty dislike for it, in love--

even when your teeth are

seething in anger with talking shit about it--

your body forgives you.

" The way you just walk in here... you are so intimidating"

My body revolted hearing that.

I would feel this eruption bubbling in the pit of my stomach--it called itself embarrassment. I used to be somewhat confused by it too--I didn't know exactly what I was doing to receive that. Merely walking into rooms or just sitting at tables. I am immediately met with that word again.

I just knew for me. I slowly started to put ice on my whiskey soul to help soothe and water down the sip of me from how I allowed myself to interpret that labeling. I wanted people to feel comfortable. I wanted people to perceive me as playful and nice because I kept feeling how wrong that labeling was.

It was the way the circumstances my body responded to that created the sense of wrongness inside of it.

Anger started to circulate within with an eye roll to support the annoyance I felt too because It happened more frequently.

observant and listening to someone--intimidating.

sitting down at a bar sipping a cocktail while I wait for a friend - intimidating

Talking about something I want to do-- intimidating

adding to a deep stimulating conversation--intimidating

I looked up the meaning on google.

I laughed when I read the actual definition because who

I am can be associated as a threat to every fucking

thing that is created to

keep me in this mundane--pussy governed--

be a dainty little flower--prototype chained to society ideologies.

It made me curious to lean into play with this lava like anger.

Intimidation can be felt by someone who can be

in a state of insecurity about their own value,

authority or inferior with one self.

You can also mislabel someone intimidating too

just from the misunderstanding of someone else's

social cues that you may not be used to.

like as innocent as shyness or awkwardness can be--

it can be off-putting and be intimidating to some.

my eye rolls turned into smiles every time I get called that

The embarrassment morphed itself into a permission slip

back to myself of how my presence can be

smelled like an aroma in the air, alerting your senses of what's near.

I turned an insult that caused a confusion swirl

of flavors into a raging compliment.

Have convos with labels that are thrown at you.

is it a threat? is it something foreign to your

 ecosystem that you may not be used to?

be your strong willed self

be your boundary, vivacious self.

be your electric stricken, assertive self

it may be alarming or disturbing to some

to see you wear it on like a strong perfume..

allow people to get headaches from the

smell or want to be devoured by you.

Intimidation is a gift to your power

There are many names for a god

Remember one of them is your own name

The entire world will tell you to label yourself and
to detail who you exactly are as if identity is a
fitted pink blazer
They forget to tell you that identity is
about discovering the continuum of
what it means to be in the total exploration
of ourselves-- moment to moment. The " I don't know"
is the G-spot to curiosity. Finger away.

your whole life gets

to be your love life

What is the most tender part on

your heart that doesn't want to be said out loud?

that tingle, that statement, that sound-

allow it to exist right here --

allow life to live through you

Your art is not up for debate

its something that is asking to live outside of you

as a pulse that carries its own electromagnetic field

to be devoured raw.

nothing is the same after that

detach from being known for it

and make the art that is gasping to be known by you

The greatest scent a woman can wear is

her own pussy juices on her wrist,

her neck; during any cycle--its life giving life back

I like myself most of the time

Maybe its the sadist in me,

maybe its the story maker in me that prioritizes

the long gravel, dirt road of distance

from not liking and liking myself that keeps

my muffled fears alive and well fed

maybe I'm terrified to look at those dislikes

and form red lipped kisses out of them.

maybe these dislikes are where blooming deaths await for me

to see that they weren't actual dislikes at all--

they are where I still romance hostility

like a tight rope for... because dear God,

I allow myself to be an all consuming

source of love; what does that say about me now?

That somehow for stories sake--

I can overwhelmingly like and dislike myself

to the bone

neither are a weight, more like complex, rigid mountains
that I travel on
and set my tent to ponder the gnawing whispers of
bypasses I have tried to shield down my own self from me.
I want to put the shield down and makeshift it into a pillow
I want to not just conveniently love me,
I want to be in the arena of both
and know they get to stimintalously live
because liking myself most of the time
is the way I experience the world through me
and maybe the vice to this is actually grace
to my all knowing humanness
its okay to not always be fond of yourself
get filled up on grace and find the art in the loudness of your
distastes.

Make a home out of you

Anger can feel like an explosive volcano--oozing its hot self onto everything --if you lean in, you can hear it's whisper
" I love you so much to allow you to be filed down like a nail on a finger."

Anger= the statable love for yourself

I am no longer intrigued to see how much

blood I can bleed as I cut my wanting body into pieces

on a cold, grey operating table stitching myself back

misplaced like I am Frankenstein.

How many self help books have I consumed

and ripped up the pages to cover my skin

in thinking and hoping the ink will

seep in and make me a god of healing?

it leaves my stomach empty

leading to binge like a feen to what else I can get rid of.

I don't want to cut and erode parts of me anymore

I desire to sit in the muck of me

Dear you, dear me-- let us remind ourselves that

being a romantic to oneself is the tending to

and being in the action

of nurturing and nourishing ourselves open.

If you look at your closet and think to yourself, " I can't wear that

long, ruffled dress with the deep v neck or that blazer with body

jewelry" or " I don't remember buying this

particular bright colored top...

they all belong to an occasion."

Remind yourself-- you are the occasion. the cause and effect.

The ravishing muse. The event of every season.

You are the occasion

" I desired to be good" I murmured out of my mouth as I sobbed with Avril Lavigne's I'm with you blasting while driving to get my partner from work. Singing the high note of. " I'm with you" feeling guilty for even belting that out because it didn't feel like I was with anyone, not even myself. Hours before, I lovingly had a sexual experience with a woman.

It wasn't my first time.

It was my first time accepting my decision in the moment to embrace it as it was.

I talked to my partner about this all, he encouraged and supported me in allowing myself to explore and: date women.

This serene, beautiful, doe eyed, dark brown haired woman who allowed me into her depth knew about my relationship too.

I was so into her and I.

As I'm still driving, scanning my body and crying, It clicked like a seatbelt --ironically the only thing in the car holding me in this loud truth.

I enjoyed it.

no.. I loved it so.

All the ideologies hitting me-- I felt like I cheated.

I felt ashamed for loving it so much.

I felt guilty for desiring it more.

And it was something I never experienced before on such a deepness.

How her and I held each other after. We both cried because it was such art--abstract, healing, sexy, mouth giving.

fully enraptured from my toes to past my head and into the ethers or some shit.

That also made me guilty because I didn't want to tell my previous partner to almost make him feel he never brought me that type of astounding pleasure when that isn't true at all. This was different not in a comparsion way-- I was thinking for him instead of allowing him to speak for himself with all this coming through me.

I picked him up,

it was a silent drive home,

we got to the house

I tried to compose myself but I completely froze like I was caught in honey--stuck, couldn't move, glued to my guilt.

I told him.

biting the tip of my tongue

we sat together, I thought I deserved some type of scolding.. I was waiting for it.

He was so proud of me for honoring myself.

I started to feel angry because I guess I desired him to tell me, " bad girl, how dare you"

he kept holding me instead.

reassuring me and wanted to know if he can hear more of what I experienced because he was in awe with the liberation I gave myself.

I wasn't bad.

and somehow that made feel relieved and somewhat sad because I really desired to be punished.

Punished--I was used to not being able to be myself without thinking how I can be the most digestible. I wasn't used to honoring myself so profoundly in all of myself, in my truth of my sexuality and the space to possibly hold more lovers.

here I was.

glistening in my freedom, dripping from being so surrendered and pleasured-- all these triggers coming in for observation because I opened the jar called, " honor yourself"

The beautiful thing, I got to be held, heard and corrected.

knowing that these were all beliefs I put on myself around relationships wrapped with other opinions of them. I get to allow my partner to talk for himself.

this desire to be good.

to whom? being good carries so many attachments, ideologies--- it can even create a people pleasing response in your nervous system.

I got to terrifyingly re-examine the " be good" theory of me.

It doesn't make you bad or wrong for desiring another partner or wanting to play within your exploration that comes with sexual identity.

Communicate, be with the discomfort, understand your boundaries.

It's okay to walk into moments and become yourself in them to be able to fully experience no matter where it goes.

be in them as they come (pun totally intended)

Let curiosity and creativity seduce you

If you didn't follow through with that innate idea,
lover or business as you imagined
you still allowed yourself to be in the
tending to of curiosity within that moment
You still attempted to jolt yourself into it
You still allowed yourself to not deny possibility
You allowed yourself to move
It's not all about following through
Sometimes it's about the orgy of play and allowance.
How brilliant you are to get curiously drunk on the moment

You are everything

You are nothing

and you are anything-- all at the same time.

Can you watch yourself slowly, as you remove your own clothing from your yearning, goose bumped body in a full length mirror?

Hold yourself right there

Can you see where you are eager to keep that certain piece of clothing on because it may feel uncomfortable to reveal that part of you?

Hold yourself right there

Can you hold your naked, full belly and caress it?

Hold yourself right there

Can you gently take your fingertips over your stretch marks and scars and whisper love notes there?

Hold yourself right there

Can you take in the smell of your natural skin scent?

Hold yourself right there

Can you lick a body part that is calling for your tongue to be on by you?

Hold yourself right there

Can you scratch your inner thigh to send a tingle to your womb?

Hold yourself right there

Can you nibble on a part of your body that craves the sinking of your teeth to be officially marked by you reclaiming your aliveness?

Can you really look at your body, enticed, with the slowest eye contact in the mirror and maybe just holding it and admitting you don't love this part yet--that gets to be where your inquiry starts to seed itself.

I dare you to eye gaze with yourself and

allow your body and gestures to tell you it's song.

***when I meet myself in the mirror, in my gaze, I tried every way to not actually look at myself. Letting myself get distracted because I didn't want to admit that I didn't like my full woman body or how I spoke to it.. the love that shows up a lot for me, are my tears or my fist might want to hit a pillow or a couch-in other moments; its slapping my own ass and having my fingers drag across my thighs--they are all ways I can love myself by allowing the fluidity of expression to be there. ***

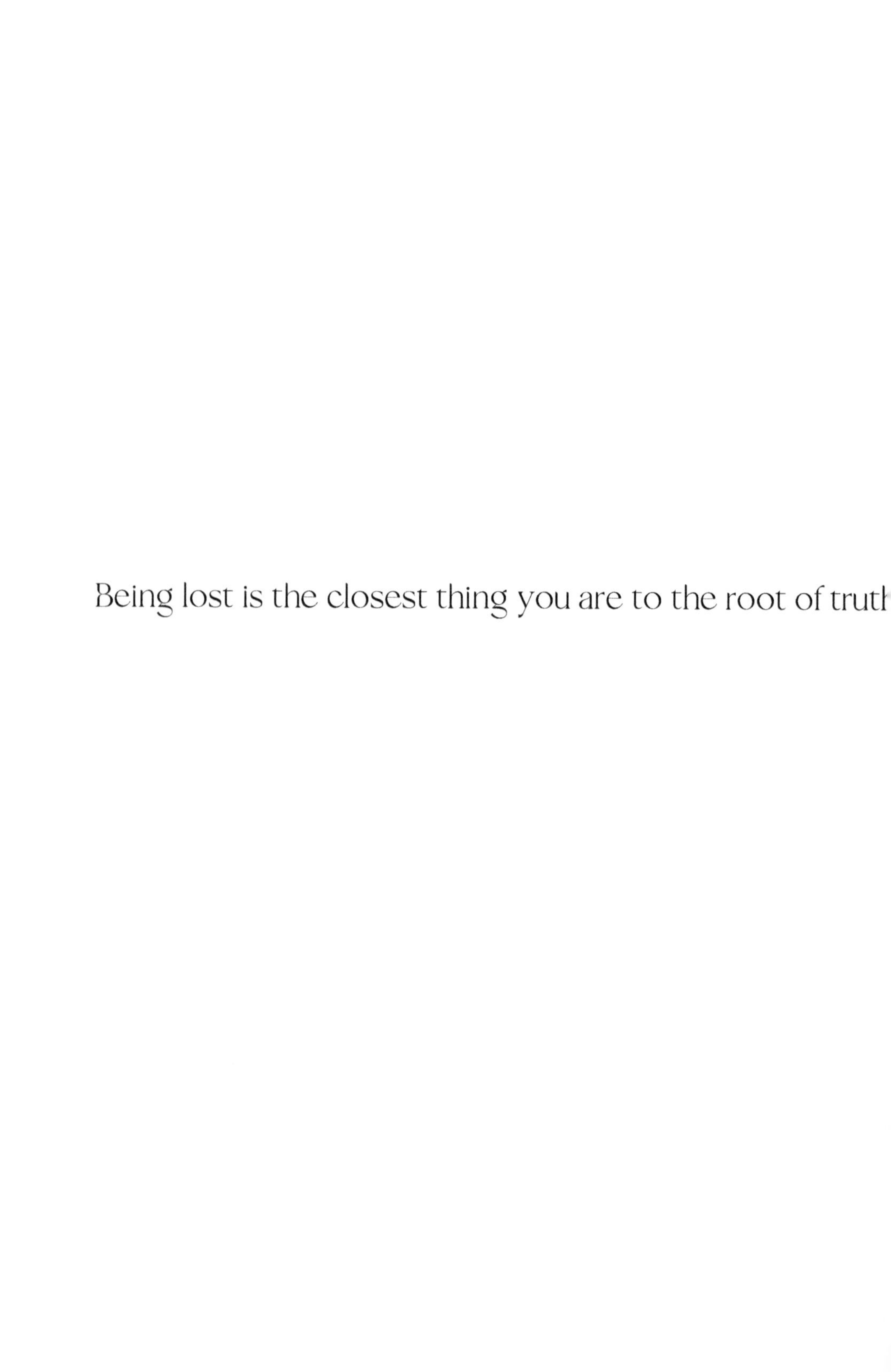

Being lost is the closest thing you are to the root of truth

What if half assing is apart of the practice?

What if half assing isn't about doing enough but an actual

 'dip your big toe' into the pool water

to get yourself to swim in the river of curiosity itself?

In etymology " half assed" means partial & it

originates from the British expression

" I can't be arsed" meaning. " I can't be bothered".

in the dictionary of slang & unconventional English

(1937) it was known as " in complete" or " not serious".

It has also been linked to the word haphazard

which defines as " no order, plan nor direction"

I used to say this phrase " I can't half ass anything

because I have a full ass" as true as that is, it was a

clever way to

desensitize my own self to my relationship with my

own fallibility. I didn't want to trust those imperfect

 rumblings that

cater to the intimacy that wanted be shared out.

What if trusting the no direction of where an idea goes is
the direction?
Half ass it
please.... be the experimenter
leave the worlds eyes hungry for more with how you play
in your imagination,
your writing,
your artistry.

even when the moon is a lemon wedge, it's still the moon.

Even when you half ass, it's still you and you romance your
fallibility whole
and give clearance to experimentation to roam.

Everything is interchangeable

your boundaries

your convictions

You may contradict what you were about

that's apart of you letting go the genesis that lives within

and allowing your own evolution and discernment to nestle

itself in for your movement of life

 it's okay to gather the research, the notepad and then put it

out and adjust as you go

The need for perfection or the permanence is what makes

the grim reaper erect

because desiring those out of anything causes a slow,

seducing death

Good ol adjustment

Blooming overpriced flowers and big balloons that spell out

" Happy mother's day" in every grocery store I entered and

 I feel this seldom sunken feeling in my heart. My womb

still remembers the phantom heartbeat of you. It rings through

my whole body like an echo. Mother's day is. where my grief

plays out its symphony. That's the thing about grief, it doesn't

go away, you learn how to move with its shape as it

comes in like a sharp wave.

II full years have gone since I miscarried and just

like grief guts you open, it also embraces you

whole again too. Grief doesn't abandon, amplifies

what you can hold.

This sounds so weird to say and It has taken me

II years to witness the gift the misscarriage was for me.

all the tears

the confusion

the influx of mixed blue & purple hues of grief.

All the pondering questions of what a kaleidoscope of a human you would be.

what your laugh would sound like.

what kind of things you would be hyper-fixed on.

how you look when you are sleeping.

Learning the world through you-I didn't know they were compost for me.

It birthed me into myself, allowing the vacant mother within to be

awoken to reparent me.

Mother's day can be such a sensitive-capitalistic--disguised as

empowerment-reminder of what you haven't experienced yet or what you have

been trying to make happen but it's not easy--kind of a day and

it makes all the sense why it does.

It also makes all of the sense to still be in the in-between: questioning the journey of

motherhood because you may have realized that

you never gave the space to answer it for yourself. Without it

being stuffed down. glamorized as this high

achieving thing that makes you the ultimate women.

And I think it's so brave you are self advocating your own choice to be childless.

You still are a woman and it doesn't dent the capabilities

you possess or the love you can feel for another human.

You are valid in that.

May you remember that you are a mother, even

if this beautiful baby didn't make it earth side, your womb

remembers its fragmented soul.. place your hand there..

you are still a mother.

.

May you remember you are still a mother, even if you are
welcoming or have been getting to know the inner mother within.
You are still a mother.

May you remember you still have a mother even if she isn't
here anymore, she becomes the earth, the nature, the howling trees,
the subtle wind that runs through your hair, the
whispers underneath the melody of songs, the quotes
that grace your eyeballs unexpectedly
when you scroll on your phone. She is still your mother.

May you remember the electricity of the coercing feminine that
lives within you, always.

call on her to be witnessed,
to be held,
to be spoken to..

Mother is listening.

Can you hold me?

even when the silhouette of shame covers

half of me and the last thing I want is for you

to look at me

" I miss you" I said as my lips quivered.

sitting in the middle of our brown couch, looking at him, fidgeting with my snake ring, to try to hold back tears because I didn't expect that to come out.

I gazed quickly up and looked at him in his eyes from across the room in the yellow chair.

he said " I miss us too"

It's as if there was 500 miles between us but here we were, in the same room.

I didn't want to ruin my makeup, we were about to leave to go on a date, the first one in a little since our schedules have been opposite and I've been diving into myself.

I couldn't hold them back

He couldn't either.

his head in his hands

I came over to ask if I could hold him,

I wrapped my arms around him and allowed my fingertips to lightly go across his back

We cried together

it was so messy

and beautiful and sad.

we kept holding one another and hearing each of our intense pining of:

" I'm tired of second guessing where to take you."

" I'm tired of the pressure to think I have to come up with everyhing"

" Why don't you confide in me like you used to?"

we competely let ourselves bleed.

We got ourselves cleaned up.

Went out for that dinner.

No phones unless it was to take photos/ videos of us or our delicious food.

We stayed for 3 hours. sitting at a dimmed high top table at this new Italian place.

copious amount of basil pizza.

holding each other's hands as we talked and laughed.

my body tingling and my heart so warm.

Don't hide from these moments of discomfort. It's apart of intimacy.

allow them to lubericate your throat and your heart to open and

break from your own diluted stories.

to bare witness to him

to get ready and them completely becoming an open mess.

to reveal to him and to myself.

to choose to get ready again and go out to dinner and be in this love of ours--

it's poetry.

it's art.

it's death.

it's being fully and utterly here.

Remain open
when your body wants to tense up,
when your heart wants to close and
wrap itself like a barbed wire fence,
When your gut says, " resist"
Remain open
Being open is the full experience
no matter what comes from this
Grant it movement until it reaches symbols that
get to be words and capitalize on
hearing the sound of it
Remain open

J'ai Envie de plus de toi
' 1 crave more of you'

You brought me to your altar.

water flowing.

Flowers were blooming out of chest.

" worship me", you whispered

Red lipstick smeared; a marker of where we began.

and on my knees... I went.

Succulent kisses.

Wallflower playing in the background

synced up to your breath.

You had me speaking in tongues; your favorite.

My fingers and lips--baptized.

Coding of your ancientness all over your pulsated,

shape shifting body and my salivated mouth.

Lingering in every drop of your nectar.

memorized by your innocence

as you let giggle.

Our bodies merged; a temple of devotion.

fuck..

I feel god here.

Wild Woman

Ooh wild woman

do not dismantle your mud

and your rock together crown.

leave those leaves, twigs and flowers upon your messy hair.

you've been told about fairytales

how when you are poise and wait to be rescued,

you seem to have this lightbulb of light within.

They didn't tell you about how your soul and emotion

embody Mother Nature with her own chaotic storms.

They didn't tell you-- you are siren who sings the songs of her

experiences with angst, passion and chaos.

they didn't tell you to wait until a materialistic item--a glass slipper

fits just right, you then, have purpose.

poise, a glass shoe and no other being is your savior.

For you wild woman,

you have been barefoot,

born to the forest and unbound to anything that doesn't speak

danger.

danger in the way it feels familiar.

danger that feels safe because you know

you aren't made to be just dressed

up and bow to distorted kingdoms.

danger challenges you

it awakens the wild, the whore and maiden within.

awareness flows through your blood.

belonging to everything and nothing--a serene, eery complex.

having the hands of an ancestor and nurturer.

the aura of a witch, a healer and a weirdo.

carrying the soul of a radical, motherly, lover.

embodying the experiences and teachings of all who have come

before you.

evoking the all of the elements: a earth, fire, air, water, nature

within you to dance

together gently to be apart of your DNA.

You are brazen.

You are layers of depth.

You are versatile.

You are a muse.

You are sex.

You are unbound.

You are darkness and void.

You are birth and death.

You are unwritten.

in the purest form.

Forge in the earth,

you wild woman

that this life is yours for the living.

Making room for all the other women who come after you.

Show them your sensuality, your teeth, your paradox and illuminate

yourself in the sacred ground.

Whenever you feel out of place,

get barefoot,

call back the elements, earth and the forest,

feel the leaves or a flower and place it in your palm

remember all that you are---wild in essence.

If the mind feels as crowded as an elevator

go outside and collect things.

a rock,

maybe a random, sun-kissed bottle cap

you flip over and see a stupid, simplisitic quote.

a random bird feather.

maybe a sunset,

a bush full of colorful flowers.

maybe laughter from a conversation you pass

by and you can't help the smirk etch a sketching

on your face.

find the art in your surroundings

aliveness lives there too.

May you remind yourself that the capacity you

have been stretching within,

is not to only hold more pain in that space

its for more love.

its for more joy too.

It's happening again,

I stop touching my flaky skin,

I don't remember when I washed my face,

I ignore the stench of my 4 day old sweatpants,

I can probably make a delicious fried egg out of the oil of my hair.

The back up generator of my energy is all out--

I don't desire to move

I forget that going slow gets to be the regeneration

I forget that water can nourish me

How good a cooked meal can taste

and how the smell of freshly lit candles gives breath to a place

The lotion I caress and lather so smoothly and lightly on my body

as I stare at my nakedness in the mirror as I go limb by limb

my leg on the bathroom counter

The texture of my skin and its origin of growth

my belly full

The thickness of my thighs

I used to take the comment as 'thick as trees' as an offense

Trees withstand and hold and root where they are

just like our feet and legs and thighs

they all have held me

When I don't even want to hold me

I'm continuing the practice of self care

seeing my patterns

all these parts of who I am

My grandmother's necklace carrying her ashes arrived today.

In a silver big oak tree.

Showcasing the roots

and the dirt.

I envisioned her somewhere green,

in her garden next to a big tree.

She grew so many things--memories

Elvis blasting in the kitchen as she moved to the rhythm on

her checkerboard floor with the occasional cop radio on as she

cooked and told me random facts about old cars.

Belly-laughing from overfilling the blender as we

 made chocolate milk shakes to go with our

 re-run marathon of the golden girls

Every time she picked me up from school, she

held my hand as she drove

and would turn up the radio, reminiscing of what

memory a song connected to.

Anytime my doll--I still have it in my room now;

I can't muster up the courage to throw it out.

It reminds me too much of you.

Her weird, funny and generous soul

I kept boundaries as I got older and my talking to you grew slim..

You were my favorite part of my childhood.

I hear your voice singing in the background when I play

" I can't help but fall in love with you" and I

immediately have to dance

like it was, you and I twirling in your kitchen .

My grandmother grew a garden inside my heart

may she rest in one.

My nephew asked me how old I was turning

and with a scrunched up face I answered, " 30"

and he smiled wide

with an Owen Wilson "wow" joyfully leaving his mouth

countinuing with " look at how much you've grown."

It hit me right in the fruit gusher

Look at how much you've grown.

In body.

In age.

In cycles.

In people.

In places.

What a delicious triumph

I rather have a whole gallery of trying

than nothing at all

You are never alone

you have the wind,

the air,

the sun

the ground

that can carry you when

you can't do it.

give it to mother

Ferociousness lived in the womb of your grandmother

and it remained dormant within your mother

until it transferred into the egg that made you.

Born untamed and fearless.

You are the ferocity

your ancestors have been waiting for.

Dearest story teller,

I want more stories.

I want more story tellers, more poets, painters, more writers.

Less info dumping.

I'm maxed out on info.

And I don't know when you confused info as value

when value is found in

the usefulness of something.

Anything that moves us is the altar whether it shows i

tself through

our bold point pen.

I want to be wide-eyed and raw eared, leaned back or my chest

pulled forward--ingrained in what you got to say.

I'm malnourished for the yearning of storytelling.

Not the polished ones that make a point,

 not the ones you rehearse in your head before

it greets your throat--the stories that are

casted from your belly, the ones that whisper

back to you when you are trying to sleep

or your stirred heart or around a campfire

you sit at or the ones burning in your

cellular structure to be told

or on a couch with delectable childhood snacks or

when you are met with silence

and the silhouette of your best friend's face on

 the pillow next to you-- I want those stories.

The ones that are living in your bones.

You come from a lineage of stories.

You start as a story.

You end as a story.

And some die with all their stories stuck under rib cages and lungs.

And the ancient things that continue on when

we aren't living are our stories.

Dear story weaver,

I dare you to tell your story again.

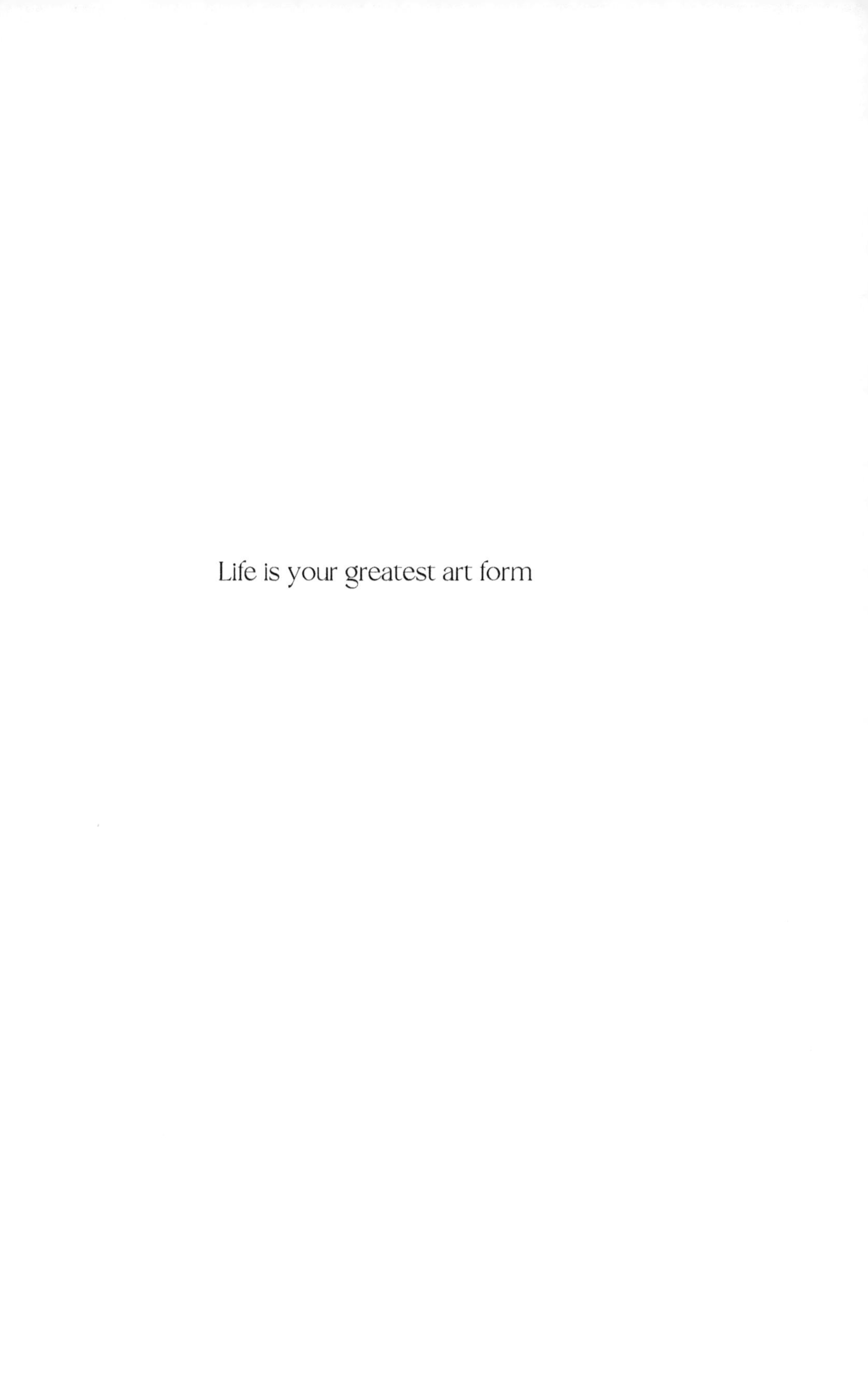
Life is your greatest art form

Acknowledgments

I want to thank my beautiful beta readers: Jessica
Jackson, Emily Louise Weber, Amanda Peden & Sara
Fox for taking the space to read my art. Thank you for
believing in me, being another set of eyes and making
my heart so full.

Thank you to Danny, my fiancee', who is the biggest
encourager and inspiration
in my writing process.
I adore you deeply.

A very special thanks to you, my readers, who have told me for years
to write a damn book after spilling my guts on the internet.
thank you for seeing something in my writing.

About the Author

Dom Demming is a writer, a bridge, a DJ, a human disco ball and a creative-intimacy facilitator. At a very young age, she turned to journaling to articulate personal questioning and the gooey in between. Her work is still a mixture of that and exploring the depths of grief, aliveness, femininity, sexual identity and ageism. She believes telling our stories can save lives even if the only life we save is our own.

'Sensual, tender, widened, messy, you' is her debut poetry collection.

Dom currently lives in Arizona with her fiancee' Danny and her cuddly and spoiled cat Freya. You can find her live, laugh and rotting on her couch with a good book or hyper-fixating on a new meal she just cooked.

where to follow her:

Instagram: @ Dom_Demming
TikTok: @Domdemming
Facebook: /DomDemming